2007 Greatest Pop and Movie Hits

THE BIGGEST MOVIES ✳ THE GREATEST ARTISTS
Arranged by Dan Coates

DAN COATES® is a registered trademark of Alfred Publishing Co., Inc.
© MMVII by Alfred Publishing Co., Inc.

ISBN-10: 0-7390-4831-7
ISBN-13: 978-0-7390-4831-3

ADELIELAND

from *Happy Feet*

Composed by John Powell
Arranged by Dan Coates

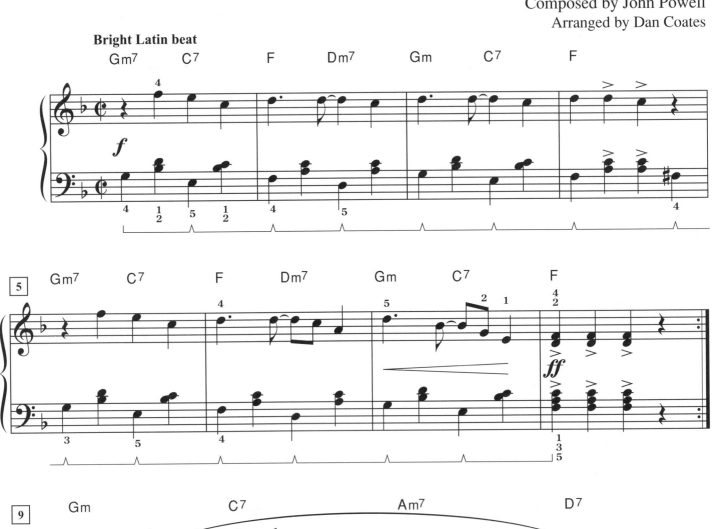

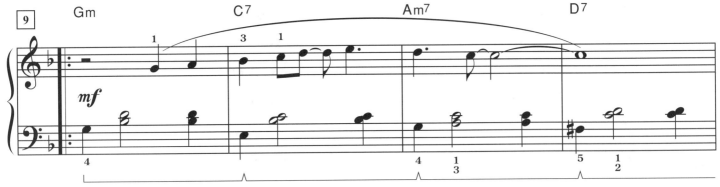

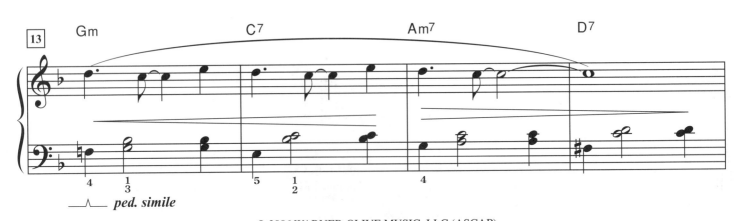

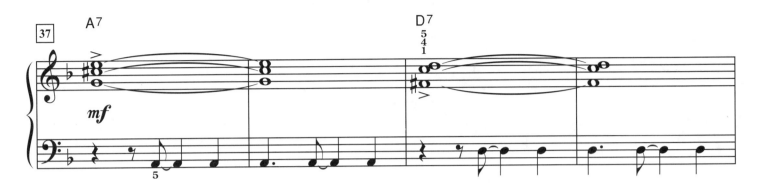

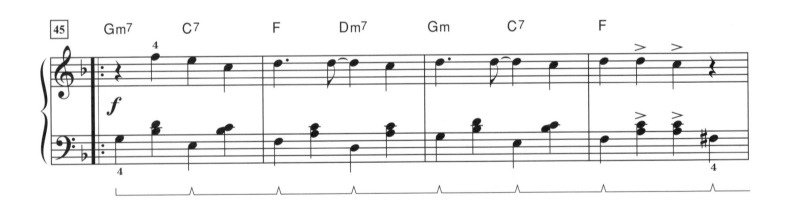

CALIFORNIA

from *The O.C.*

Words and Music by
Al Jolson, B. G. DeSylva, Joseph Meyer,
Jason Schwartzman and Alex Greenwald
Arranged by Dan Coates

BILLY'S THEME

from *The Departed*

By Howard Shore
Arranged by Dan Coates

CAN YOU READ MY MIND?

from *Superman Returns*

Words by Leslie Bricusse

Music by **JOHN WILLIAMS**
Arranged by Dan Coates

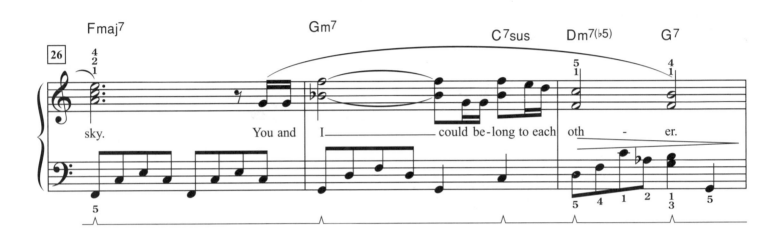

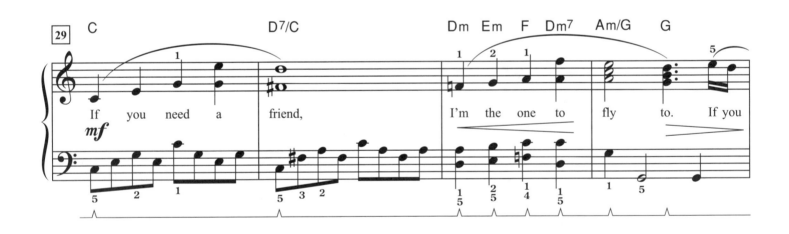

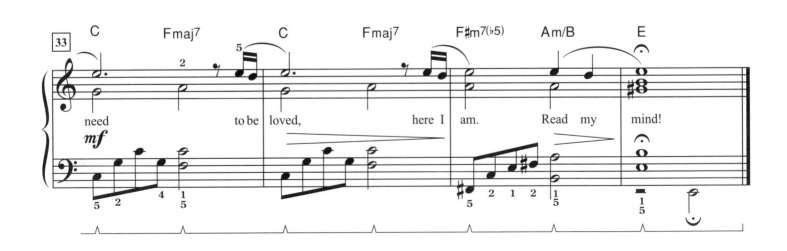

CHASING CARS

Words and Music by
Gary Lightbody, Nathan Connolly,
Jonathan Quinn, Paul Wilson
and Tom Simpson
Arranged by Dan Coates

Moderately, with a steady beat

Verse:

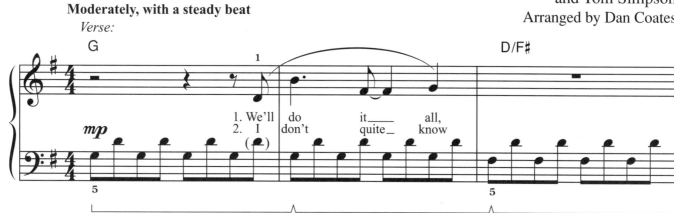

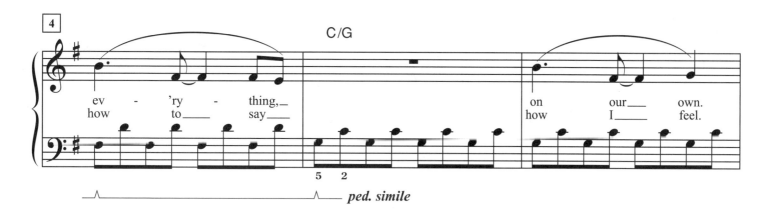

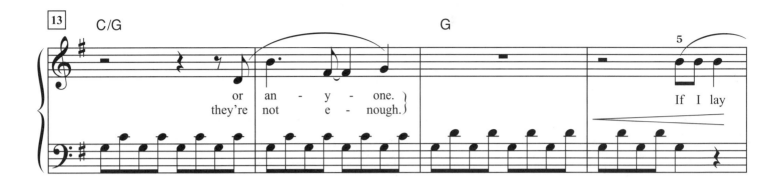

or an - y - one.
they're not e - nough.

If I lay

Chorus:

here,

mf

if I just lay here,

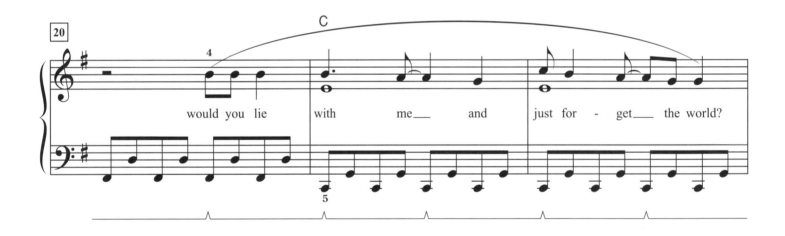

would you lie with me___ and just for - get___ the world?

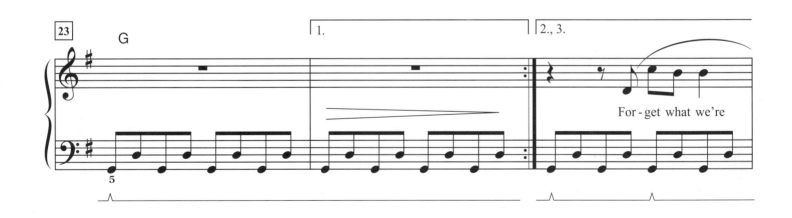

For - get what we're

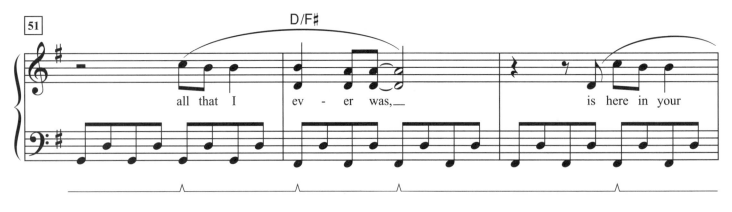

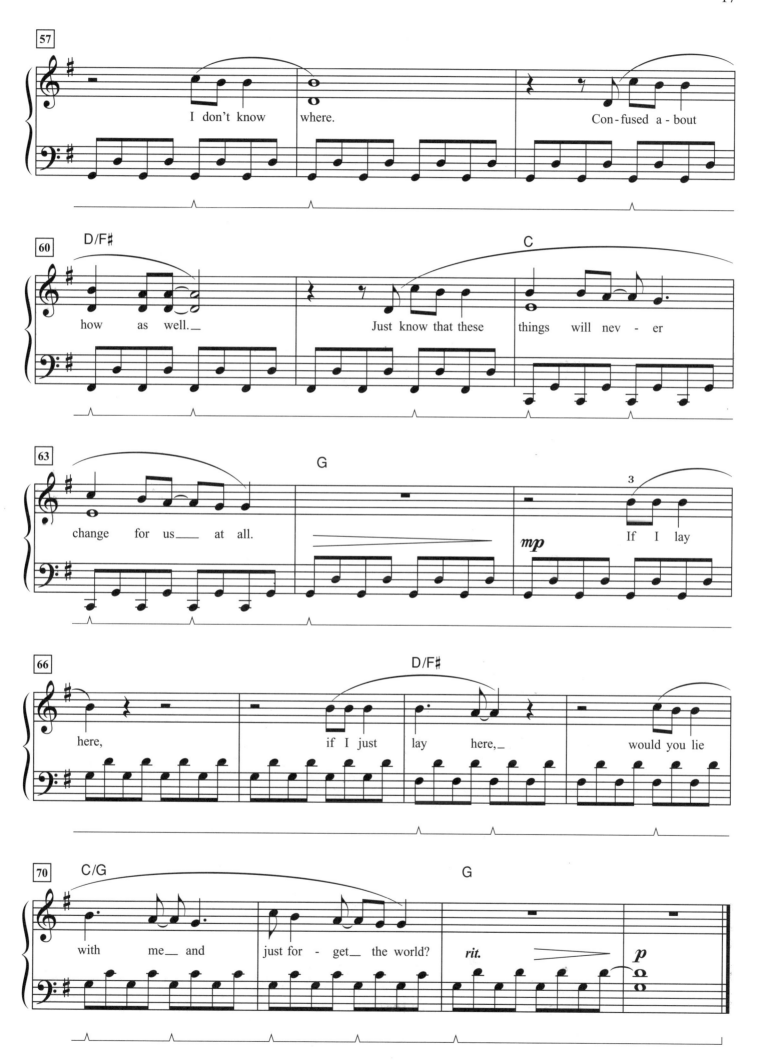

THE DEPARTED TANGO

from *The Departed*

By Howard Shore
Arranged by Dan Coates

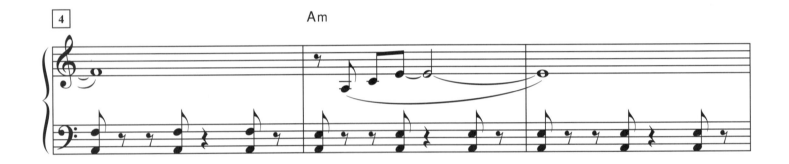

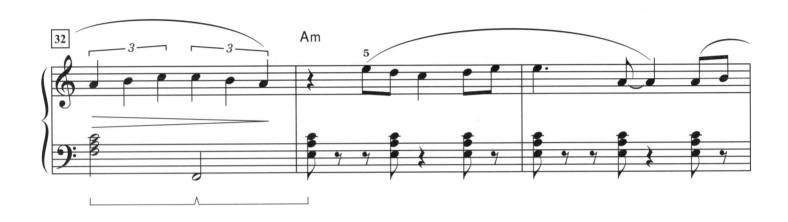

GONNA FLY NOW

from *Rocky Balboa*

Words and Music by Bill Conti,
Ayn Robbins and Carol Connors
Arranged by Dan Coates

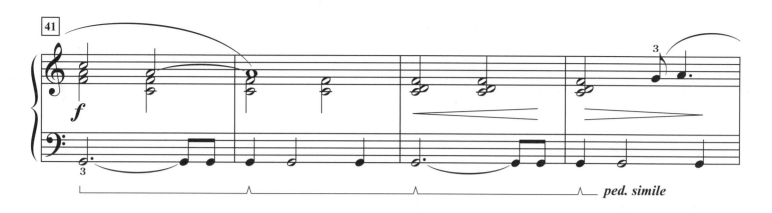

HIGH

Words and Music by
Ricky Ross and James Blunt
Arranged by Dan Coates

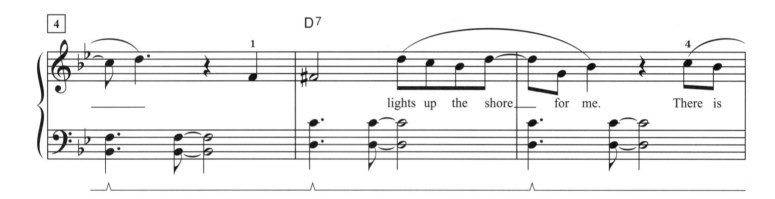

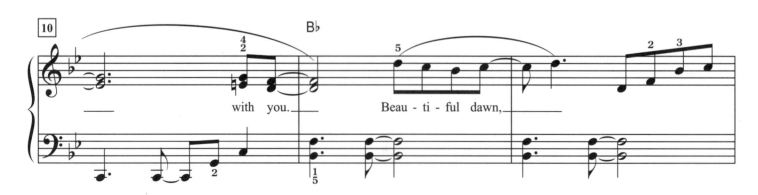

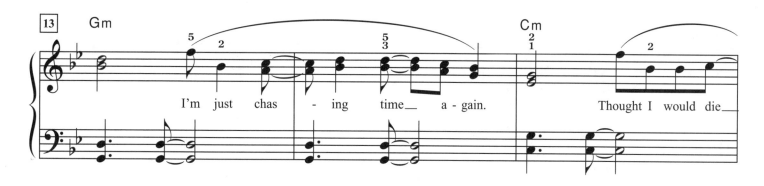

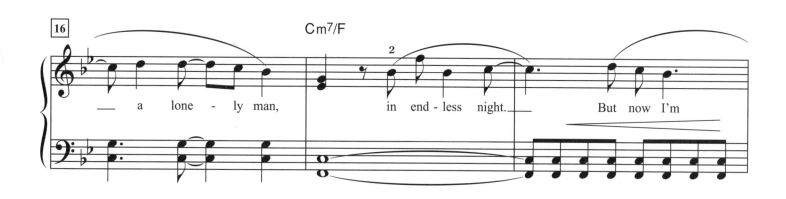

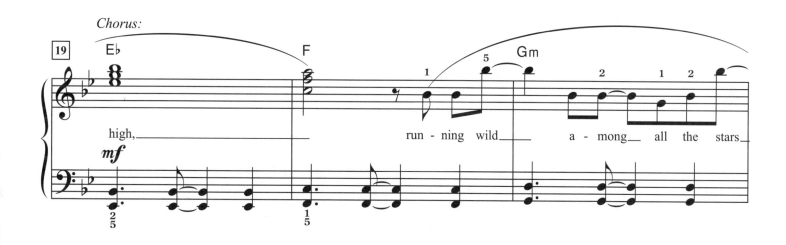

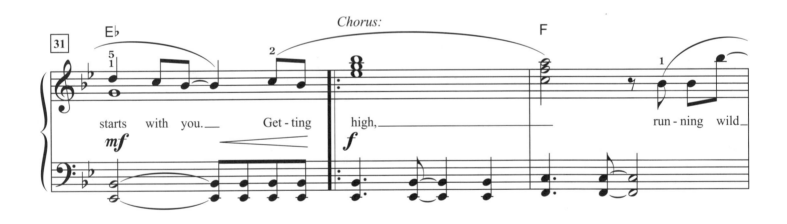

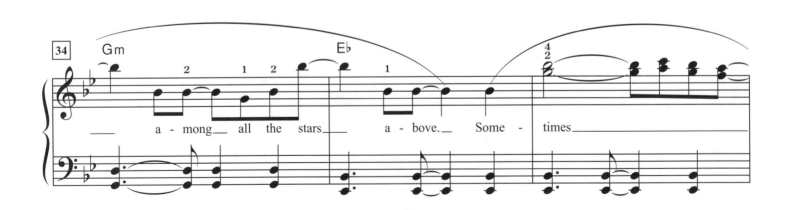

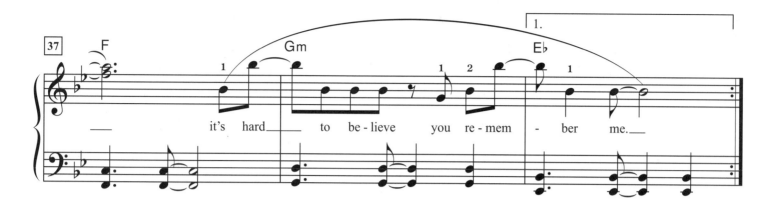

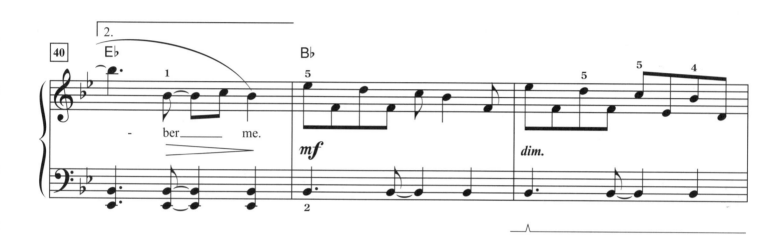

Verse 2:
Beautiful dawn,
Melt with the stars again.
Do you remember
The day when my journey began?
Will you remember
The end of time?
Beautiful dawn,
You're just blowing my mind again.
Thought I was born
To endless night,
Until you shine.
(To Chorus:)

I BELIEVE IN YOU

(Je Crois en Toi)

Words and Music by David Kreuger,
Per Olof Magnusson, Jorgen Elofsson,
Matteo Saggese and Luc Plamondon
Arranged by Dan Coates

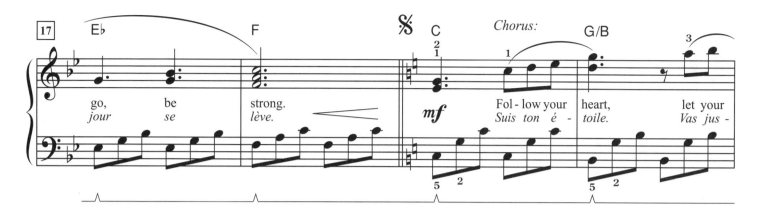

17

E♭   F   𝄋 C   *Chorus:*   G/B

go,   be   strong.   *mf*   Fol - low your   heart,   let your
jour   *se*   *lève.*   *Suis ton é -*   *toile.*   *Vas jus -*

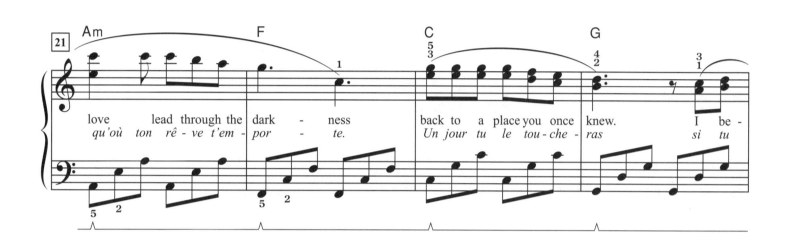

21

Am   F   C   G

love   lead through the   dark - ness   back to   a place you once   knew.   I be -
qu'où   *ton rê - ve t'em -*   *por -*   *te.*   *Un jour tu*   *le tou - che -*   *ras*   *si tu*

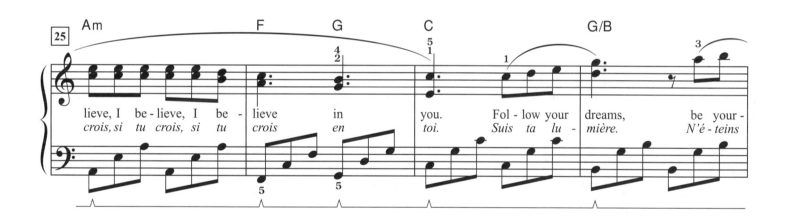

25

Am   F   G   C   G/B

lieve, I be - lieve, I be -   lieve   in   you.   Fol - low your   dreams,   be your -
crois, si   *tu crois, si*   *tu*   *crois*   *en*   *toi.*   *Suis ta lu -*   *mière.*   *N'é - teins*

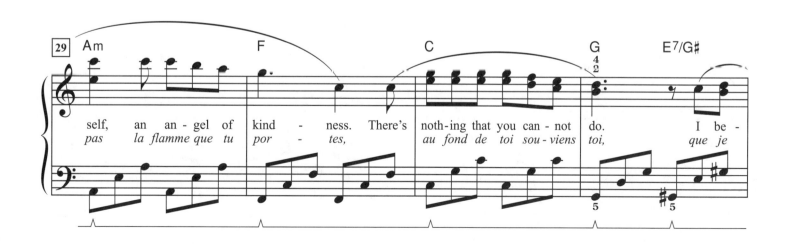

29

Am   F   C   G   E7/G♯

self,   an an - gel of   kind - ness. There's   noth - ing that you can - not   do.   I be -
pas   *la flamme que tu*   *por -*   *tes,*   *au fond de toi sou - viens*   *toi,*   *que je*

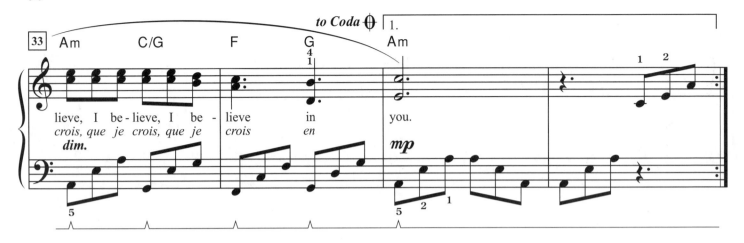

lieve, I be - lieve, I be - lieve in you.
crois, que je crois, que je crois en

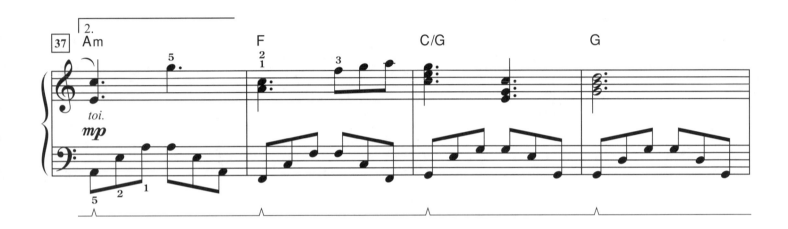

toi.

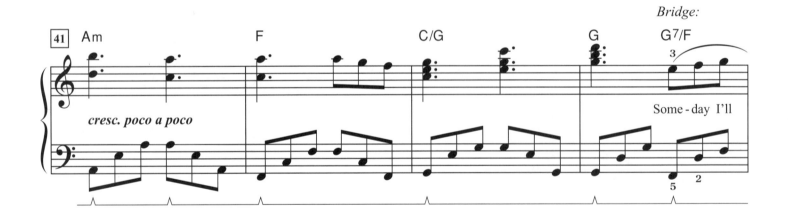

Bridge:

Some - day I'll

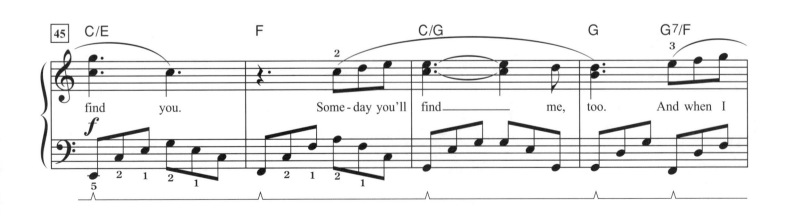

find you. Some - day you'll find_____ me, too. And when I

D.S. al Coda

hold you close, I'll know that it's true.

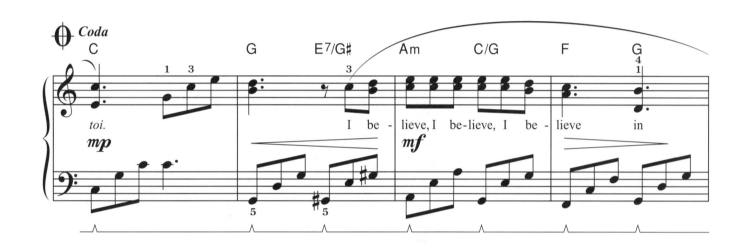

toi.

I be-lieve, I be-lieve, I be-lieve in

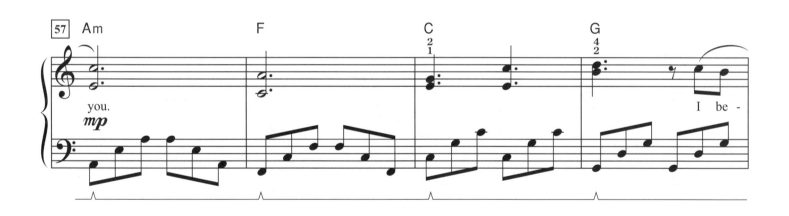

you.

I be-

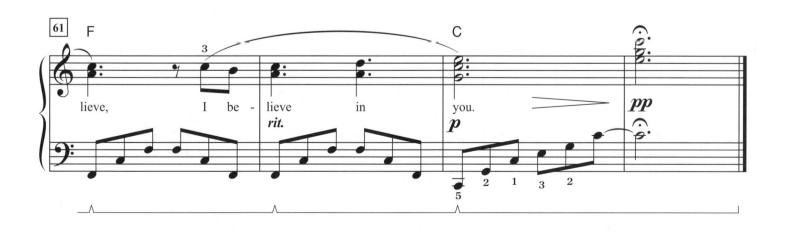

lieve, I be-lieve in you.

I KNEW I LOVED YOU

Music by Ennio Morricone
Words by Alan Bergman and Marilyn Bergman
Arranged by Dan Coates

moon - light _____ at last to - geth - er. _____ Here in the in - can - des - cent glow, we are

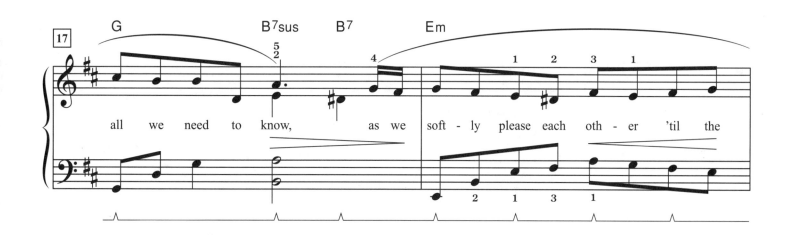

all we need to know, as we soft - ly please each oth - er 'til the

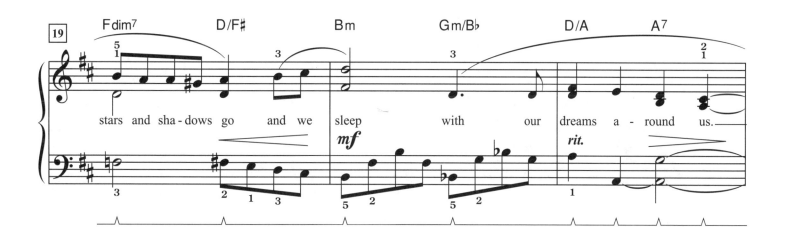

stars and sha - dows go and we sleep with our dreams a - round us.

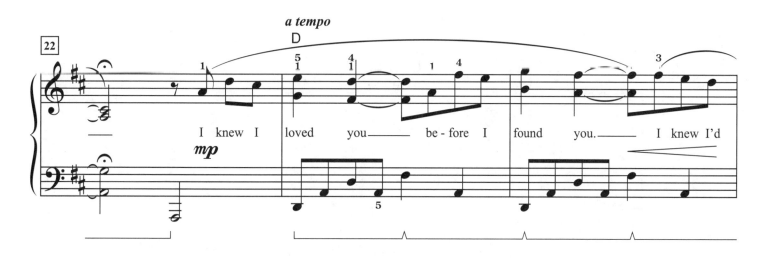

_____ I knew I loved you _____ be - fore I found you. _____ I knew I'd

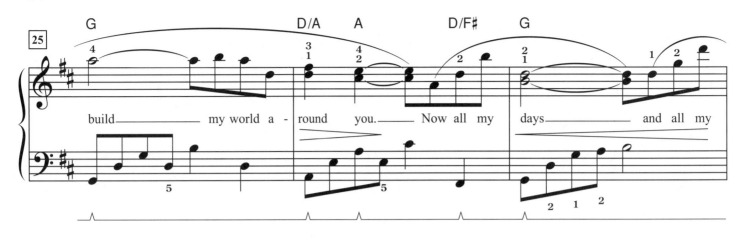

build_____ my world a - round you.____ Now all my days_____ and all my

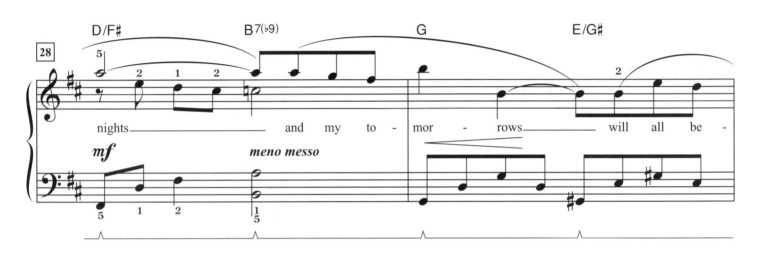

nights_____ and my to - mor - rows_____ will all be -

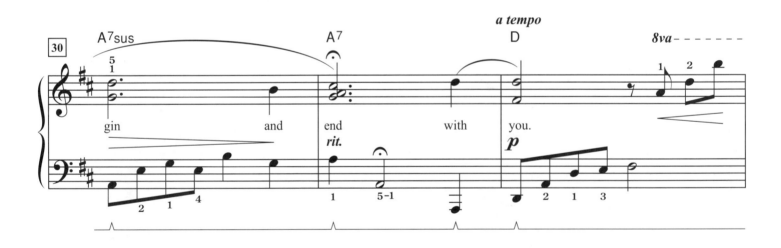

gin_____ and end_____ with you.

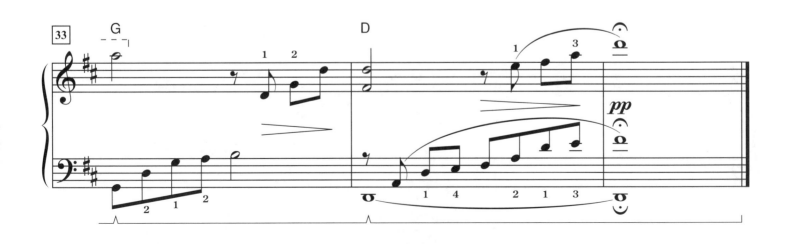

IN ROSA VERNAT LILIUM

from *The Nativity Story*

Music by Mychael Danna
Latin Poetry and Translation by Elizabeth Danna
Arranged by Dan Coates

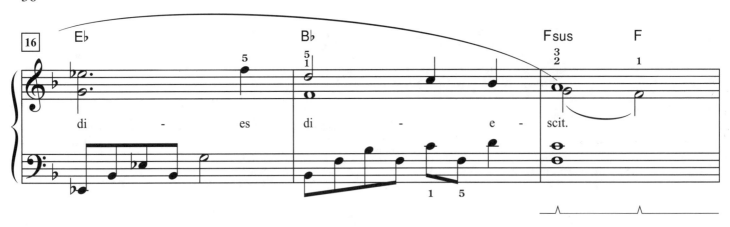

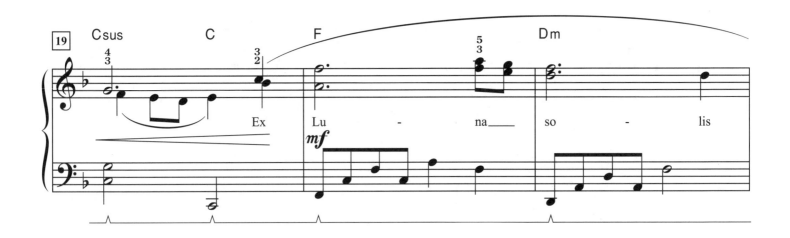

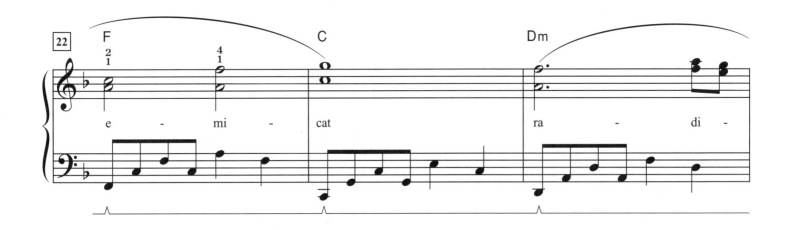

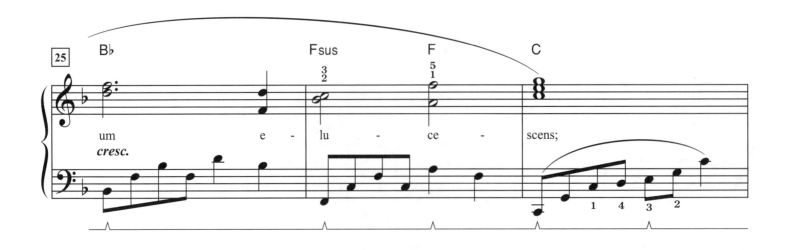

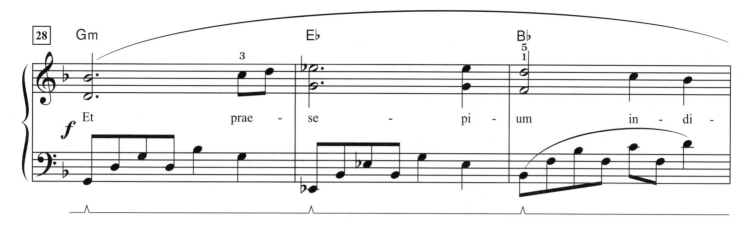

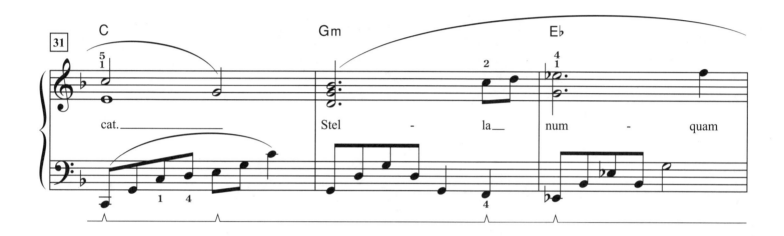

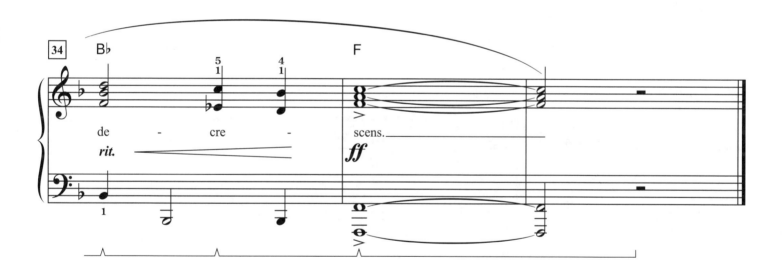

Lyrics with English translation:

In Rosa, vernat lilium	From the rose spings up the lily
Flos in flore florescit	Flower in flower flourishes
Secundum Dei concilium.	According to God's plan.
Vera, dies diescit.	The true day dawns.
Ex Luna solis emicat	From the moon shines
Radium elucescens;	The sun's brightening ray;
Et praesepium indicat.	And the star that never dims
Stella numquam decrescens.	Points out the stable.

JAMES BOND THEME

from *Casino Royale*

By Monty Norman
Arranged by Dan Coates

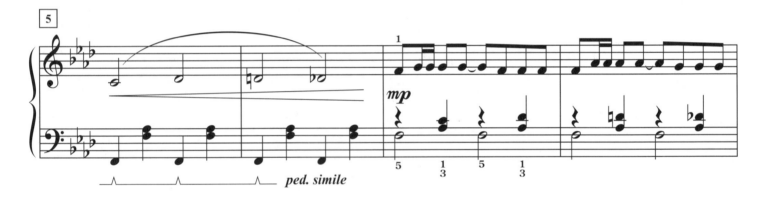

LOVE WILL ALWAYS WIN

Words and Music by
Wayne Kirkpatrick and Gordon Kennedy
Arranged by Dan Coates

THE PINK PANTHER

from *The Pink Panther*

By Henry Mancini
Arranged by Dan Coates

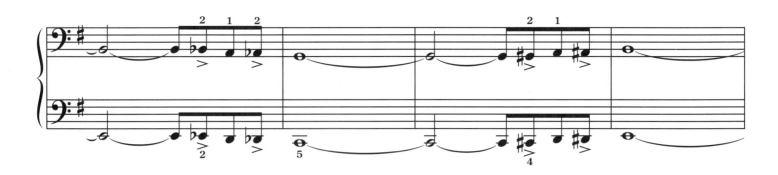

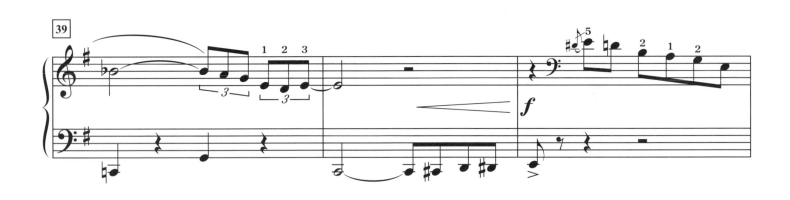

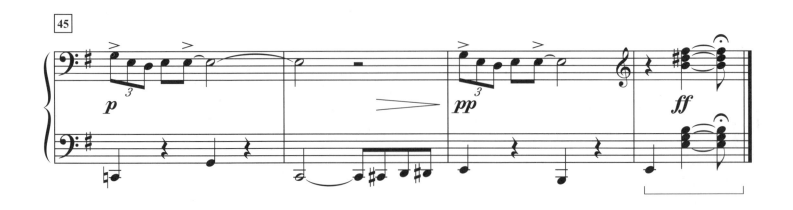

SOME HEARTS

Words and Music by
Diane Warren
Arranged by Dan Coates

Moderately bright

Verse:

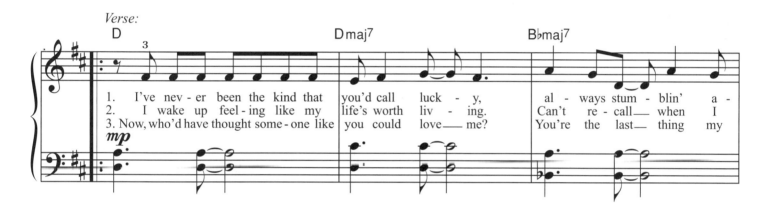

1. I've nev-er been the kind that you'd call luck-y, al-ways stum-blin' a-
2. I wake up feel-ing like my life's worth liv-ing. Can't re-call when I
3. Now, who'd have thought some-one like you could love me? You're the last thing my

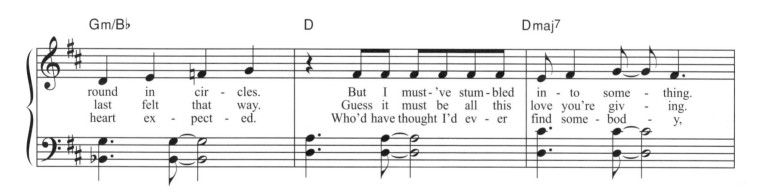

round in cir-cles. But I must-'ve stum-bled in-to some-thing.
last felt that way. Guess it must be all this love you're giv-ing.
heart ex-pect-ed. Who'd have thought I'd ev-er find some-bod-y,

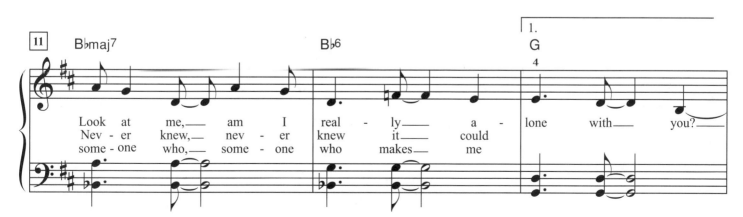

Look at me, am I real-ly a-lone with you?
Nev-er knew, nev-er knew it could
some-one who, some-one who makes me

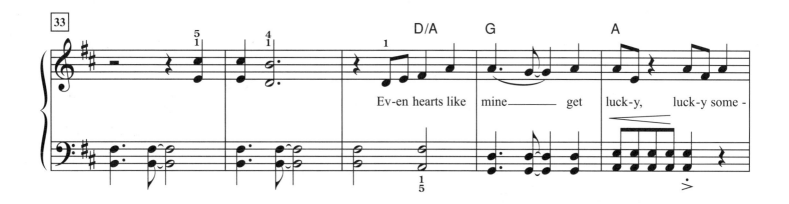

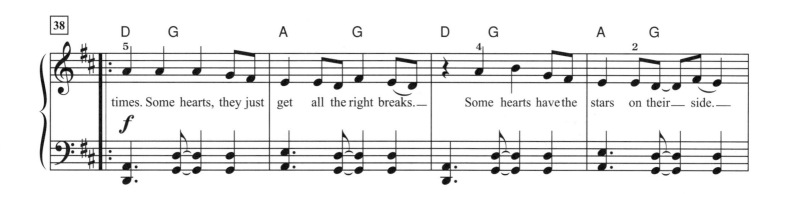

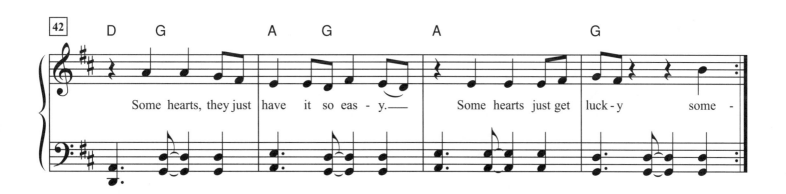

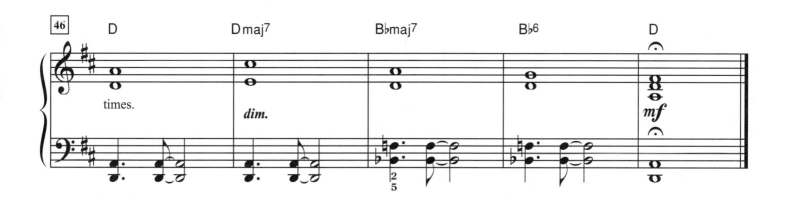

SILLY DREAMER

from *The Sweet Dreams Movie*

Lyrics by David Goldsmith
and Andy Heyward

Music by Andy Street
and Andy Heyward
Arranged by Dan Coates

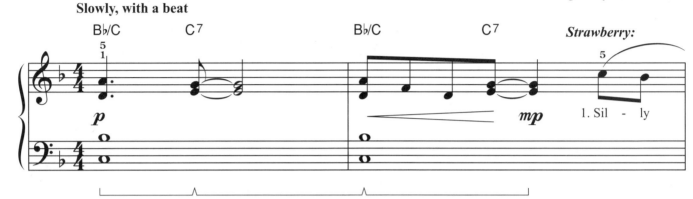

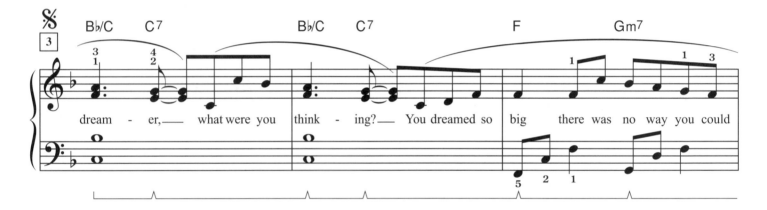

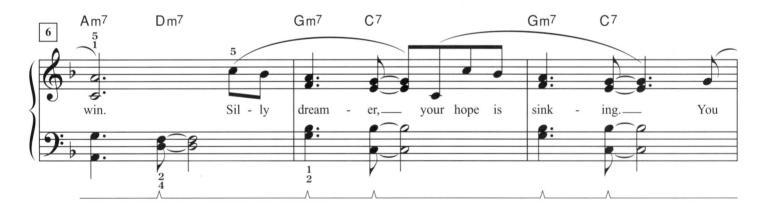

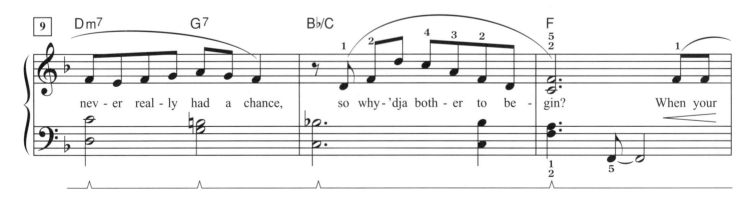

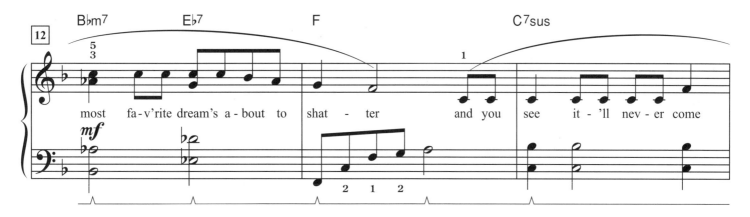

most fa-v'rite dream's a-bout to shat - ter and you see it - 'll nev - er come

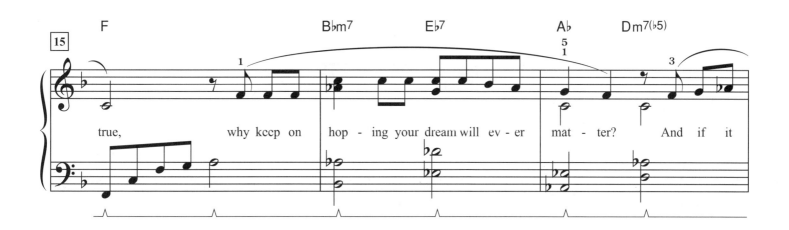

true, why keep on hop - ing your dream will ev - er mat - ter? And if it

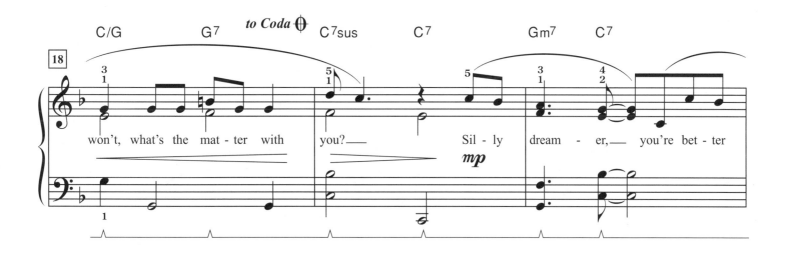

won't, what's the mat - ter with you?___ Sil - ly dream - er,___ you're bet - ter

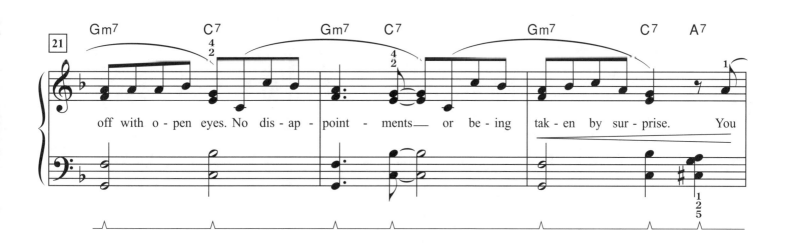

off with o - pen eyes. No dis-ap - point - ments___ or be - ing tak - en by sur - prise. You

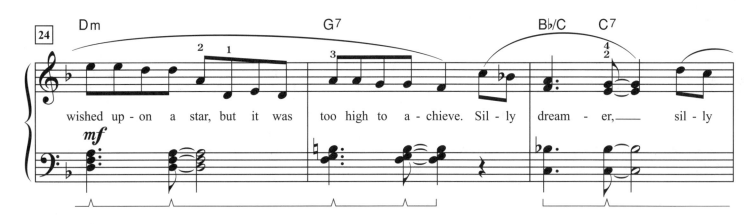

wished up - on a star, but it was too high to a - chieve. Sil - ly dream - er, ___ sil - ly

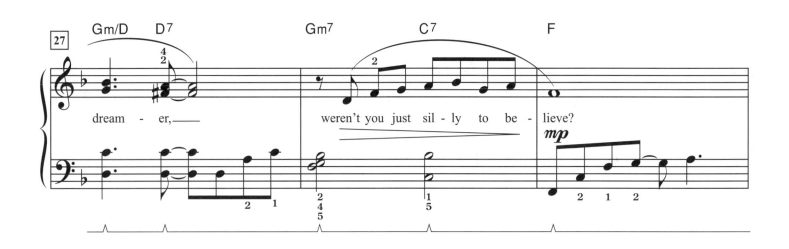

dream - er, ___ weren't you just sil - ly to be - lieve?

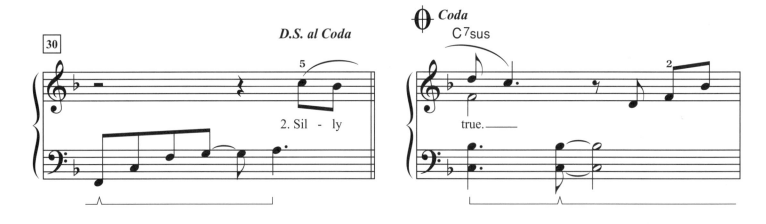

2. Sil - ly

true. ___

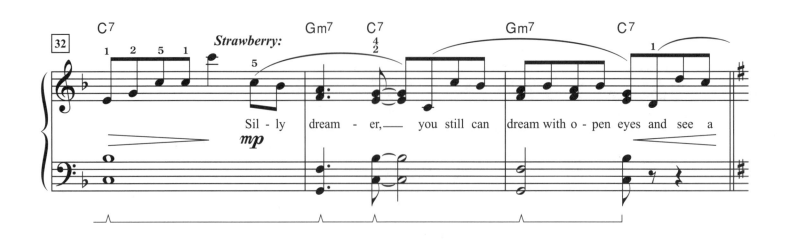

Sil - ly dream - er, ___ you still can dream with o - pen eyes and see a

Verse 2:

Ginger: Silly dreamer, don't stop your dreaming.

Orange: No dream's too big and no victory too small.

Angel: Silly dreamer, it's you who leads us.

Lemon: Without our dreamers,
How on earth would we get anywhere at all?

All: When it seems like you ought to stop believing
And it feels like there's no more you can do,
Just hold on, knowing darkness is deceiving.
With the light, all your dreams may just come true.

STRANGER IN A STRANGE LAND

Words and Music by
Barry Gibb, Ashley Gibb and Stephen Gibb
Arranged by Dan Coates

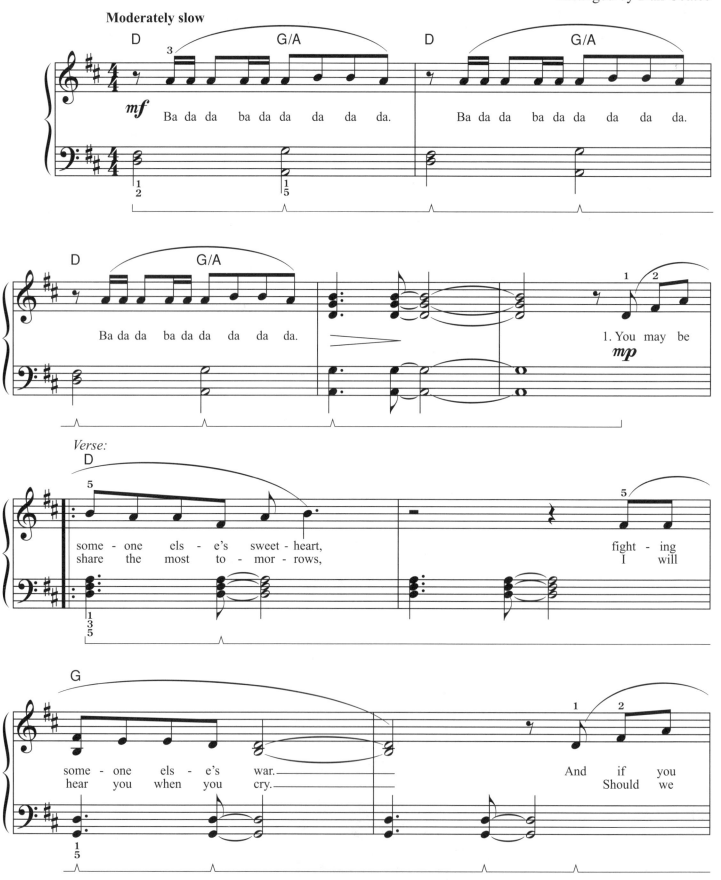

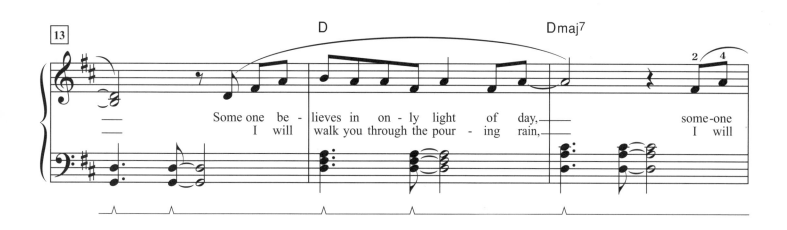

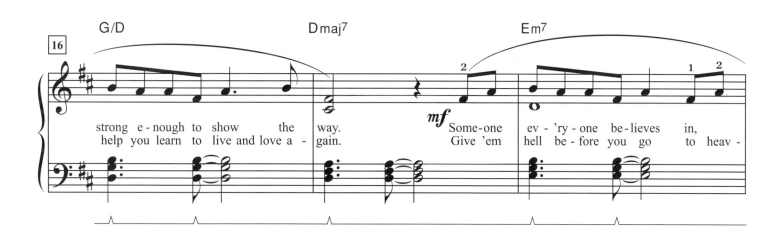

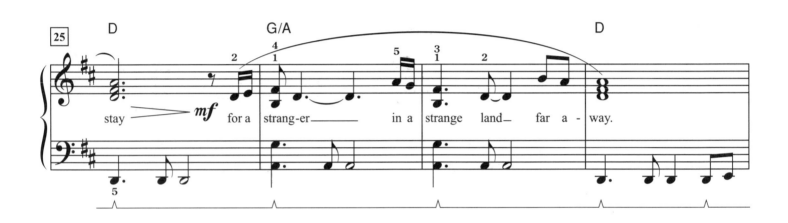

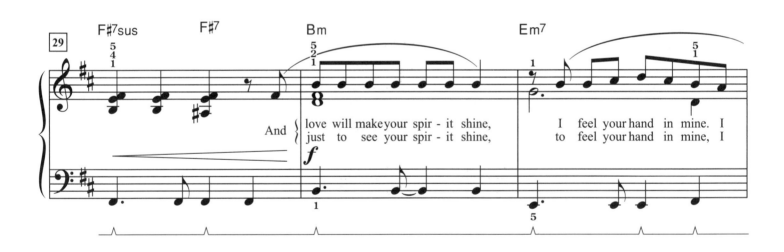

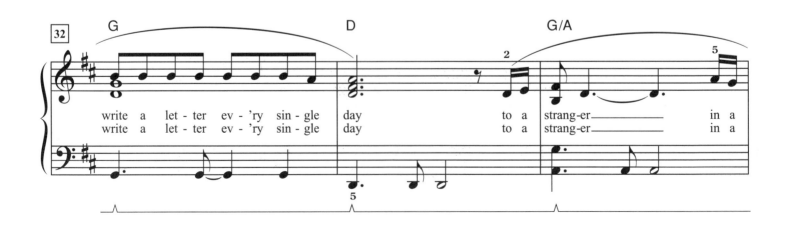

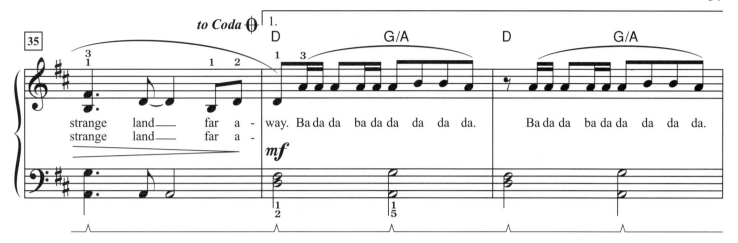

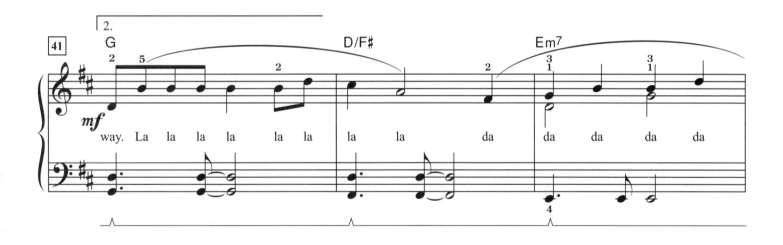

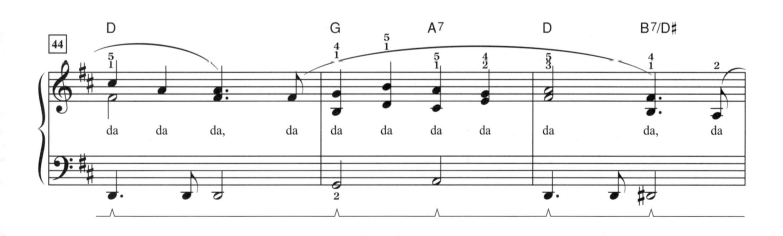

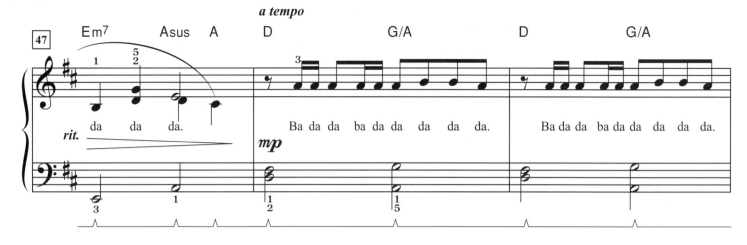

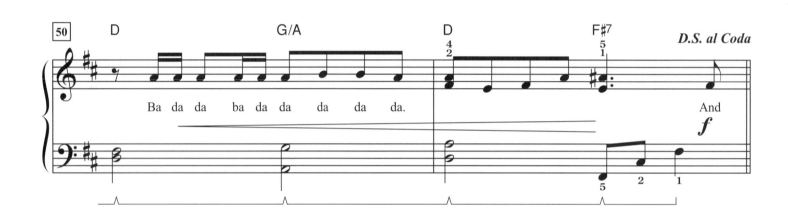

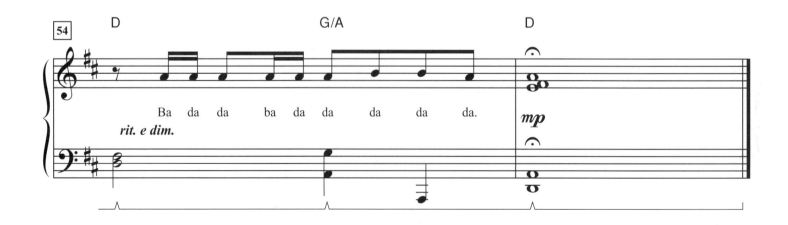

SUPERMAN THEME

from *Superman Returns*

By **JOHN WILLIAMS**
Arranged by Dan Coates

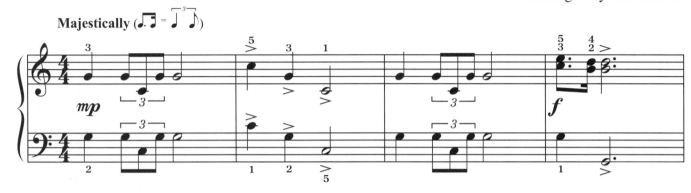

Medium march tempo

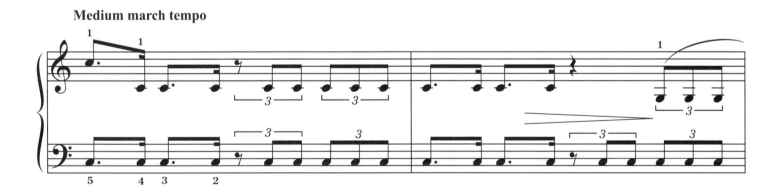

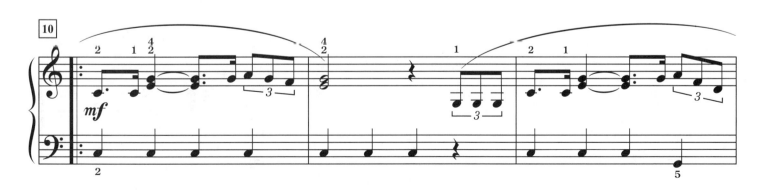

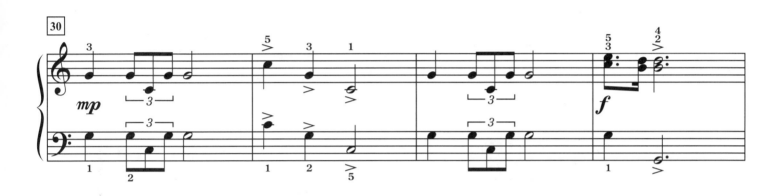

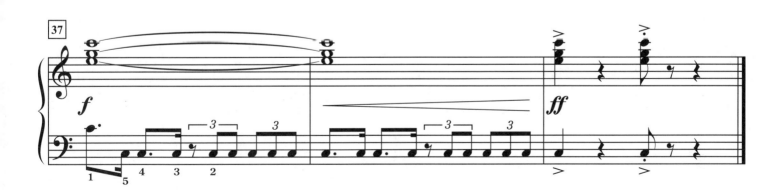

WAY BACK INTO LOVE

from *Music and Lyrics*

Words and Music by Adam Schlesinger
Arranged by Dan Coates

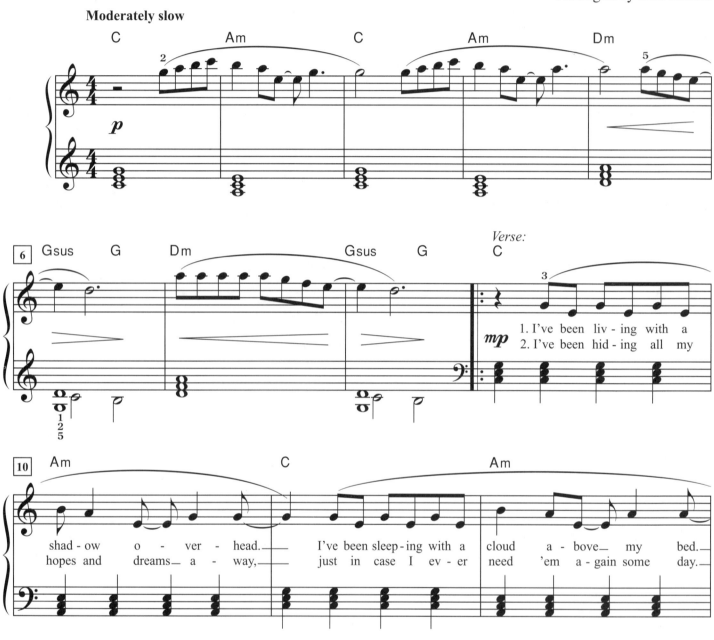

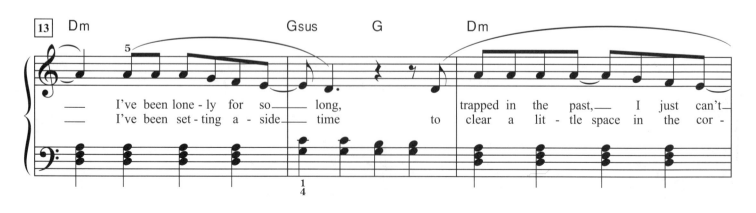

Verse 3:
I've been watching, but the stars refuse to shine.
I've been searching, but I just don't see the signs.
I know that it's out there.
There's got to be something for my soul, somewhere.

Verse 4:
I've been looking for someone to shed some light,
Not somebody just to get me through the night.
I could use some direction,
And I'm open to your suggestions.

(To Chorus:)